Your Amazing Itty Bitty™
Discover the Power of Living a Purpose-Filled Life

15 Steps to Health and Well-Being
Inspired by Ayurvedic Principles

Gigi Santiago MS, AP

Published by Itty Bitty™ Publishing
A subsidiary of S & P Productions, Inc.

Copyright © 2024 **Gigi Santiago**

All rights reserved. No part of this book may be reproduced or transmitted in any form or by any means, electronic or mechanical, including photocopying, recording, or by any information storage and retrieval system, without written permission of the publisher, except for the inclusion of brief quotations in a review.

Printed in the United States of America

Itty Bitty Publishing
311 Main Street, Suite D
El Segundo, CA 90245
(310) 640-8885

ISBN: 978-1-959964-95-7

This information is for educational purposes only and is not intended as a substitute for medical advice, diagnosis, or treatment. You should not use this information to diagnose or treat a health problem or condition. Always check with your doctor before changing your diet, altering your sleep habits, taking supplements, or starting a new fitness routine.

Dedication

My son Gabriel has shown me that God's plan was already set in motion. I am grateful and honored to be his mother, and I thank him for molding me into the woman I am today.
I love you. XOXO Mama

I extend appreciation and gratitude to my guru-deva for her unwavering support throughout our journey together. From the moment we met, you have been a constant in my life. Thank you for the invaluable lessons and instrumental guidance throughout my healing process.

With gratitude to all my yoga teachers who have guided me along my journey, I express deep appreciation to their teachers and gurus.

Stop by our Itty Bitty™ website to find interesting information regarding Discover the Power of Living a Purpose-Filled Life

www.IttyBittyPublishing.com

Or visit Gigi Santiago at

https://www.b3vedaspirit.com/

Your Amazing Itty Bitty™ Discover the Power of Living a Purpose-Filled Life

15 Steps to Health and Well-Being Inspired by Ayurvedic Principles

Do you want to find more happiness and fulfillment as you journey through life? This book is inspired by Ayurveda, a practice focused on balancing the body and mind. It offers different techniques and therapies based on a deep understanding of how the body works and the connection between the mind, body, and spirit.

In Her book, *Your Amazing Itty Bitty™ Discover the Power of Living a Purpose-Filled Life,* Gigi Santiago offers essential steps to rejuvenate and repair your body while actively helping you maintain a sharp mind.

You will learn to:

- Connect with your true inner self
- Acknowledge and cultivate your strength
- Focus on the challenges you face
- Set clear expectations
- Achieve seemingly impossible goals

To achieve paramount outcomes on your journey to healing, pick up a copy of this informative and enlightening Itty Bitty™ book today!

Table of Contents

Introduction
Step 1. Transforming a Purpose-Filled Life
Step 2. The Simple Act of Resting
Step 3. The Transformative Power of Gratitude
Step 4. Between Alertness and Perception
Step 5. Overcoming Obstacles
Step 6. Ritual for Self-Care
Step 7. The Range of Active Silence and Rest
Step 8. Keys to Healthy Habits
Step 9. Ritucharya: Seasonal Change
Step 10. Breaking the Cycle
Step 11. Unlock a New Level of Happy
Step 12. Cultivate Inner Strength for Positive Change
Step 13. Exploring Abhyanga for Health
Step 14. You Are Freaking Perfect
Step 15. Ayurvedic Principles and Optimal Health

Introduction

Life is a thrilling adventure toward the ultimate destination of happiness! Your existence has a higher purpose: to expand happiness and fulfillment as you journey through life. With every step you evolve and grow, becoming more intelligent, powerful, and creative. The natural process of evolution leads to the expansion of everything meaningful in life—a truly beautiful thing. The key to a healthy satisfying life is striking the right balance between rest and activity.

- Resting is essential for rejuvenating and repairing the body, while activity helps maintain a healthy body and sharp mind.
- Think of life as a dance, moving and grooving, then take a breather to soak in the moment.

So, embrace life's journey with open arms and see it as an exciting and exhilarating process of growth and evolution toward the ultimate goal of happiness and fulfillment!

With love and gratitude,
Gigi

Step 1
Transforming a Purpose-Filled Life

To live life to the fullest and keep your mind and body in top shape, you must find a balance between rest and play.

Did you know that Ayurveda, an ancient Indian system of medicine, can help you achieve complete and balanced nourishment?

According to Ayurveda, it's not just the physical substances you consume that matter, but also the mental, emotional, and spiritual experiences you digest. This holistic approach to nourishment can help maintain a healthy mind-body system and lead a more fulfilling life.

1. The art of mindful eating is true therapy for your tummy! By relishing your food in a peaceful environment, you can help your gut break down nutrients like a champ.
2. Mindful eating also includes chewing more, eating slowly, appreciating your food, and eliminating distractions.

The Ayurvedic Secret

Dinacharya is all about syncing natural rhythms of the day and seasoning with a balanced diet, regular sweat sessions, and self-care habits that pamper you like royalty.

- Start with a daily meditation practice to create a harmonious mind-body connection and feel in sync with your true self and purpose.
- Establishing a regular and early bedtime is essential for optimal health.
- Experts recommend going to bed between 10:00 and 11:00 p.m. and waking up between 6:00 and 7:00 a.m.

Improve your well-being through twice-daily meditation to reduce stress levels and establish a stronger connection with your inner self. Plan one session in the morning and one in the evening for maximum benefits.

Step 2
The Simple Act of Resting

Have you ever felt stressed out and uncertain about what to do next?

1. Practicing meditation might just be the perfect solution for you!
2. Meditation reduces stress and provides clarity with a deeper understanding of your thoughts and emotions.

Taste buds are the gateway to inner intelligence, as they allow you to uniquely experience and connect with the world.

1. Taste is essential for your well-being, enriching your sensory experience and fulfilling a fundamental need for vital energy.
2. Taste can be a distraction and can be used as a tool for a mindfulness approach to meditation to enrich the experience.
3. Meditation is the most powerful tool to connect with your inner intelligence, leading to spontaneous action in all areas of life and reexperiencing the soul.

The Trifecta of Conscious Thinking

By exploring your mind through meditation, you can tap into your inner wisdom and gain more clarity and focus in daily life.

- Consciousness is an undeniable aspect of self-awareness in nature.
- There's a three-in-one consciousness structure (self-awareness) in the statement, "I know myself," consisting of the observer, the observed, and the relationship between them.

We relate the wholeness of nature to the soul, mind, and body.

- Your identity reflects your soul, which expresses subjectivity and the ability to witness.
- Your mind is the container for all emotions, perceptions, thoughts, feelings, and desires.
- Your body is not simply a shell; it's a rather powerful embodiment of your personality. By maintaining physical well-being, you amplify your inner qualities and project an even stronger sense of self to the world.

Step 3
The Transformative Power of Gratitude

Growth is an innate life process achieved by striking a balance between periods of rest and activity.

1. During the growth process, it's normal to experience distress or discomfort.
2. Practice meditation with compassion and gratitude. Be mindful of discomfort.
3. Keep in mind that it is perfectly acceptable to take a break or seek support when needed.

The Power of Being Present

Meditation is where the mind is both relaxed and energized.

1. Take time to appreciate things you often overlook; calming your mind has great power.
2. Gratitude for everything you have is the key to experiencing true happiness.

Brain Health Influences Conscious Experience

Your spinal cord transmits sensory information to your brain, and motor information to your body.

- Its main structure and function is the autonomic nervous system (ANS), a network that regulates involuntary body processes.
- The spinal cord has three divisions: the sympathetic, parasympathetic, and enteric nervous systems, maintaining perfect balance between infinite silence and infinite dynamism in reflexes found in the deep contemplation associated with meditation.

The synapse is vital to your nervous system, a bridge between cells, allowing electrical information to travel from one cell to the next.

- External factors such as air quality and diet can significantly impact your environment, brain, and peripheral nervous system.
- Environmental factors, actions, and surroundings can cause changes that impact gene function, leading to disease.
- Understanding your relationship with food and rest is crucial to controlling disease progress and for developing effective treatments.

Step 4
Between Alertness and Perception

Comprehending the dual phases of meditation involves two distinct stages: inward and outward strokes. The inward stroke involves exploring the hidden depths of knowledge and understanding, which are not yet manifested. Examples are focused breathing with eyes closed, while the outward stroke is concerned with its dynamic nature and what physically sutrounds you in the world.

1. Your level of alertness, memories, and experiences influence interpretation of information within your consciousness.
2. Consistency in your meditation practice can reveal the power of integration and progression.
3. Meditation integrates and advances your life, allowing you to navigate challenges and reach goals. It's like a coin with two sides: introspection and practical application.

The Thalamus: Sensorimotor Processing

The thalamus plays a crucial role in processing sensory information by determining appropriate destinations in the brain. Additionally, it receives output from the cortex and effectively directs it to the corresponding spinal cord and peripheral tracks.

- The thalamus is also responsible for governing states of basic awareness or arousal.
- It is also a discriminating central structure for all input and output.

Maintaining a delicate balance in neuronal communication across the synaptic gap is extremely important. This gap is like a bridge enabling communication via special chemicals to expedite messages between cells. The thalamus reliably prevents disruption caused by genetic, dietary, environmental, and behavioral factors, ensuring that balance is effectively maintained.

Step 5
Overcoming Obstacles

Regular observation of self and inspiring compassion within yourself and others are crucial qualities you must possess to accomplish your divine purpose.

1. Divine purpose is not random; it follows a specific pattern. The universe operates in a precise orderly manner. Divine purpose reflects the same organized systematic approach.
2. Living with a sense of divine purpose can kindle a spark within to bring an elevated level of creativity, fulfillment, and meaning to life.
3. Purposeful living promotes self-sufficiency and alertness, creating an unstoppable force.

Holistic-based consciousness is the use of mind-body therapies. This is a comprehensive health system comprising methods that invigorate the body's inner intelligence and balance its physiology.

Mind-Body Therapies

Holistic medicine emphasizes treating the whole person by addressing the underlying causes of ailments, rather than just symptoms.

- Meditation techniques include breathing, mindfulness, movement, mantras, and more. Seek professional guidance for best results.
- Sound therapy uses sound and vibration to affect mind and body, including sound healing, vibroacoustic sound therapy, and music therapy.
- Vibration therapy improves muscle strength, range of motion, and blood flow. It also reduces soreness and delayed-onset muscle soreness (DOMS), ranging from tenderness to extremely painful muscle pain.
- Use UV light for inflammation, blue light for acne, red for wrinkles and sun damage, yellow for skin health, and red LED light for inflammation and collagen. You can find UV lights in infrared light therapy saunas, or from holistic practitioners trained in light color therapy.
- Gem therapy uses crystals and minerals to relieve pain, balance the mind, reduce stress, and promote self-healing.
- Get personalized lifestyle counseling for diet, digestion, yoga, herbal preparations, and purification procedures.

Step 6
Ritual for Self-Care

"Brahmamuhurta" is a daily routine in Ayurveda suggesting that the best times to practice spiritual activities such as meditation, contemplation, and other related practices is between 4:00 a.m. and 6:00 a.m. Achieving tranquility is a practice requiring time, peace, and clarity. This is a beautiful time when everything aligns perfectly: inner peace, external tranquility, and sharp memory.

1. Wake up early at 6:00 a.m. In winter's dark months, rise an hour later. Your goal is to feel well-rested.
2. Upon waking, first tend to personal hygiene by eliminating waste, washing your face, and practicing oral hygiene. You can also try oil pulling to detoxify your head and digestive system.
3. Maximize meditation by starting with a quick abhyanga (herb-infused) oil massage. Simply apply your favorite oil to your ears and feet in long flowing strokes with gentle pressure.

Tips for Healthy Meal Plans

Lunch should be your main meal of the day.

- For a protein-rich lunch, have one or two cups of cooked organic veggies, whole grains, and soy products or curdled foods like cheese, cottage cheese, or yogurt lassi, a popular drink.
- For dinner choose easily-digestible foods, such as cooked grains, veggies, or lentil soup. Flavor bedtime beverages with cardamom or ginger, or make hot cereal with plenty of water.

Skipping breakfast is not recommended.

- To increase your appetite for lunch, try stewed fruit and whole-grain cereal with ghee or olive oil.
- If you get hungry before lunchtime, add ground nuts to your cereal with milk or soy milk for extra protein.

Step 7
The Range of Active Silence and Rest

As you explore different levels of silence and rest, you can discover a wide range of activities from the universe to the smallest particles. As you learn more, your understanding of the world grows. Knowledge is always changing depending on your state of mind.

1. A multi-stage process includes thought, action, achievement, and fulfillment. Even during your daily routine, your mind can maintain a state of focus.
2. Being fulfilled means finding peace in being active. This is about finding rest within the work you do.

The Yoga Sutras, of sage Patanjali, provide a comprehensive guide to exploring the relationship between the mind, body, and spirit.

1. The sutras illuminate the mind's pivotal role in your journey of self-discovery and self-realization. They advocate for mental discipline through meditation and breath control, leading you to transcend physical limits and attain higher consciousness.
2. Some yoga and meditation practitioners believe practicing the Yoga Sutras can rewire the brain, increasing awareness and inner peace. By unlocking your full potential and a deeper connection to yourself.

The Yoga Sutras of Patanjali

The yoga sutras of Patanjali consist of eight yoga elements that promote physical and mental well-being. These elements are:

- Yama (abstinence)
- Niyama (observance)
- Asana (yoga posture)
- Pranayama (breath control)
- Pratyahara (withdrawal of the senses)
- Dharana (concentration of the mind)
- Dhyana (meditation)
- Samadhi (absorption)

The yoga sutras offer guidance for achievement of balance and harmony.

- Meditation can increase awareness and inspire positive change.
- Transformation involves moving from a natural state of being, known as Prakrti (nature, first, or original), to a state of perfection, or Samskara, which means intentional or well-planned action. This concept refers to a complete, well-made state, attained through the transformative process.

Step 8
Keys To Healthy Habits

It's important to assess your body's toxicity levels and understand that impaired digestive and metabolic processes can cause a buildup of toxic by-products.

1. Shower before you eat.
2. Eat your main meal in the middle of the day.
3. Sit down to eat for better digestion.

Unhealthy habits can promote feelings of lethargy, brain fog, grogginess, and lack of motivation. These include:

1. Feeling not fully rested upon waking in the morning
2. Physical weakness without apparent cause
3. Common colds or sinus congestion multiple times annually

Take Care of Yourself First

Sometimes, your body doesn't work as it should, whether related to breathing, digestion, elimination, or something else. It's important to listen and take notes.

- Discomfort or indigestion after meals
- Lacking desire to eat without genuine cravings
- Mental and physical fatigue, exhaustion

These symptoms should be taken seriously; you are encouraged to discuss them with your family physician. Diet and lifestyle habits can often be linked to these symptoms.

Step 9
Ritucharya: Seasonal Change

Ritucharya is a concept derived from two Sanskrit words: 'ritu,' meaning season, and 'charya,' meaning routine or discipline. This traditional practice encourages individuals to adjust their lifestyle and diet in harmony with the physical and emotional changes that accompany different seasons.

1. A year is divided into six seasons, each lasting two months. Three of these seasons are warm, while the remaining three are cool.
2. In hot weather, the body becomes weak due to qualities such as lightness, sharpness, and mobility. Cool weather has heavy dense attributes that strengthen the body.

The body requires more fuel to stay warm and healthy in the winter months. Your fire principle (appetite) is activated, and you naturally eat more.

Maintain Body-Mind Balance with Ritucharya

If not managed properly, seasonal changes can disrupt the balance of both body and mind. With the science of ritucharya, however, the body can adjust to seasonal changes.

- Seasonal changes require balance in diet and routine. Reducing and building a daily diet requires maintenance for good health. It's crucial to pay attention to what you eat.
- In Ayurveda, individuals have a unique combination of three primary doshas: Vata, Pitta, and Kapha, which influence aspects of physical, mental, and emotional well-being. They are affected by seasonal changes, so it's important to maintain a balance between them to promote optimal health.
- In Vata season (fall/winter), eat sweet potatoes, beets, and citrus fruits to counterbalance cooler weather. Cinnamon and ginger help digestion in this season.
- Pitta dosha (summer) is fiery and intense. Eat foods like cucumbers, melons, and leafy greens to pacify its nature and stay refreshed in summer.
- Kapha dosha (spring/early winter) is cold, heavy and damp. Eat berries, radishes, and leafy greens to balance sluggish seasonal tendencies.

Step 10
Breaking the Cycle

Developing your whole self is crucial for experiencing a sense of fulfillment in life. Without balance, life can feel incomplete.

1. Your toolbox of seasonal diet routines, self-care rituals, meditation, and alternative treatments is a powerful resource for breaking stress cycles and unsatisfied desires by promoting flow in your life.
2. These changes can greatly improve your quality of life, allowing you to achieve your goals and find fulfillment.

As you progress in your personal growth journey, you will develop a greater sense of tolerance and acceptance of others.

1. You'll develop a more positive mindset and strengthen overall well-being, including physical health, mental acuity, and increased self-confidence.
2. You'll enjoy diverse thinking, create opportunities, break stereotypes, societal barriers and develop cultural tolerance.

Life Stages According to Vedic Perspective

The Vedic perspective on life stages promotes good health using Ayurvedic principles encompassing age, time of day, and season.

- Brahmacharya refers to the lifestyle principles of truthfulness, cleanliness, nonviolence, and celibacy/abstinence. The first 25 years are considered a time of learning.
- Grihastha is the second stage of life (ages 25-50) when you engage with the world, community, work, family, and financial security.
- Vanaprastha is the third stage of life (ages 50-75), during which you partially retire from worldly life to focus on what truly matters.
- Sannyasa is the final stage of life (ages 75-100+). By embracing this stage, you can truly delve into the spiritual realm to attain peace and tranquility.

Step 11
Unlock a New Level of Happy

A new level of happy is not just a phrase; it's a vision you aspire to. Discover a place where you can attain happiness and contentment, where you feel safe and secure, and where opportunities are available for you to thrive and succeed. Happiness means living a fulfilling life.

1. It's important to keep your aspirations in check and work to achieve them responsibly in a sustainable manner.
2. When you come together and combine efforts, you can create a truly beautiful life that supports the growth and progress you want.

The natural order of life celebrates the coexistence of differences in harmony as the fundamental nature of existence.

1. By taking care of yourself first, you can reach your full potential and contribute to the creation of a beautiful life.
2. Recognizing your personal progress contributes to accepting and celebrating your distinctive qualities.

Promoting Peaceful Coexistence: A Call to Action

Prioritizing self-care enables you to unlock your full potential and positively impact societal growth and development.

- Practice daily dinacharya routines for the day and the evening.
- Adopt a seasonal holistic diet approach to meals to achieve a healthier lifestyle.

Further ways to promote immunity, balance, and spiritual growth.

- Daily meditation practices
- Positive activities: practicing yoga, embracing yoga ethics, utilizing therapies involving teas, herbs, and treatments

Panchakarma is an Ayurvedic treatment that incorporates five procedures to cleanse the body internally. This therapy is used for preventive healing, offering extensive therapeutic benefits that can alleviate various illnesses.

The Panchakarma treatments consist of:

- Vamana (therapeutic emesis)
- Virechana (purgation therapy)
- Vasti (therapeutic enema)
- Nasya (errhine therapy)
- Raktamokshana (bloodletting), not performed in the US

Step 12
Cultivate Inner Strength for Positive Change

You hold the potential for positive change within. By harnessing life's challenges, you fuel your inner strength and emerge from adversity more resilient and radiant than ever. Although the idea can be intimidating, adversity's silver lining allows positive change to truly shine.

1. According to Ayurveda, the state of sattva is when body, senses, mind, and spirit are in harmony.
2. Sattva reduces rajas and tamas, paving the way for liberation, vitality, well-being, and satisfaction.

Understanding sattva, rajas, and tamas in your daily life.

1. Sattva suggests wisdom born within. It inspires selfless service, purity of heart, truthfulness, and compassion for others.
2. The raja qualities are characterized by centeredness, individuality, drive, movement, and dynamism.
3. Tamas qualities can hold you back through attachments, making you cling to certain situations (confusion, anger).

Sattva: A Potential Solution for Anxiety and Insomnia

Sattva, which is designed to balance rajas and tamas energies, may be beneficial for addressing two conditions.

- Anxiety and insomnia are two prevalent conditions affecting many people today.
- These conditions are characterized by loss of sleep and increased anxiety, from everyday worries to severe disorders such as PTSD.

These conditions often manifest in daily life, challenging balance and well-being. With appropriate intervention and support, you can lead a healthy, fulfilling life free from debilitating anxiety and insomnia.

- Appropriate approaches include a combination of interventions such as cognitive-behavioral therapy, medication, and lifestyle modifications.
- Anxiety and insomnia can greatly affect life. Prioritizing self-care and seeking professional help is important.

Step 13
Exploring Abhyanga for Health

Abhyanga is a transformative treatment that profoundly affects the nervous system. It's known to calm the mind, improve all aspects of life, and lead to greater awareness and enlightenment.

1. Abhyanga, an ancient Ayurvedic practice, is a holistic approach to skin health.
2. Abhyanga has a range of skin benefits, including improved circulation, increased hydration, and enhanced detoxification.

This technique involves the application of warm oil to the body in a prescribed manner.

1. By incorporating this technique into your daily routine, you can promote optimal skin health and achieve a radiant complexion.
2. Abhyanga is most effective for skin detoxification in the morning.
3. Healing oil blends are recommended for promoting better sleep, relieving pain, and inducing relaxation.

Guidelines for Applying Oil-Based Products and Massages

- It's worth noting that skin can absorb oil, so it's best to avoid applying oil-based products after a heavy meal or when you're congested.
- Additionally, it's not advisable to get a massage during a heavy menstrual cycle, as it may exacerbate menstrual symptoms.

Incorporating this technique into your daily routine, promotes optimal skin health for a radiant, glowing complexion, enhances the immune system, and creates a natural shield to protect against negative ions and/or influences.

Below are the best oils to use based on your Ayurvedic body type:

- Vata mind/body type: ether, air (sesame oil)
- Pitta mind/body type: fire (coconut or sunflower oil)
- Kapha mind/body type: water (mustard or almond oil)

It is always best to consult an Ayurvedic practitioner before incorporating any new practices into your routine to ensure they are appropriate for your unique constitution and current state of health.

Step 14
You Are Freaking Perfect

Never underestimate the immense potential in your life. To fully actualize the value and significance of your divine purpose, it's essential to grasp its entire scope.

1. You are enough and possess immense worth and value.
2. Your soul is divine energy that remains untainted and unconquerable.

In Ayurveda, ama therapy is a crucial practice that requires a thorough examination of the ama level accumulated in the body. The appropriate way to eliminate it before treatment is recommended. The process utilizes interventions like ama pachana and agni deepana, which can mitigate the impact of ama on the body and promote overall health and well-being.

1. Ama pachana means to purify toxins.
2. Agni deepana is the practice of using spice and herbal preparations consumed before meals to aid digestion.

A Holistic Drink for Detoxification and Digestion

If you want to purify your body of toxins and improve digestion, try ama pachana, a simple hot spice water drink. Make a large batch of this detoxifying drink in the morning, transfer it to a thermos, and sip on it throughout the day.

- Two quarts of purified water
- Two or three thin slices of fresh ginger
- ¼ tsp cumin seeds
- ¼ tsp of fennel seeds
- Two black peppercorns
- Two mint leaves

Directions

Boil two quarts of water with spices. Simmer for five to ten minutes then strain and pour into a thermos. Enjoy it all day.

- Best served at room temperature
- Avoid chilled drinks

Step 15
Ayurvedic Principles and Optimal Health

A health crisis can trigger transformation along with a hidden positive message presenting an opportunity to turn the crisis into an advantage. Ayurveda helps by enhancing the immune system and alleviating some side effects.

Incorporate Ayurveda in Your Daily Routine:

1. Yoga aids in stabilizing and relaxing the body, improving concentration, memory, balance, mental acuity, and tranquility.
2. Practice nourishment with intention and a peaceful eating environment by turning off screens and eliminating distractions to fully focus on your meal.
3. Begin your day with a few minutes of deep, deliberate breathing to center yourself. Throughout the day, take short breaks to perform gentle stretches. As your day winds down, engage in a calming yoga session to alleviate physical strain and clear your mind.
4. Before bedtime, indulge in soothing meditation, concentrating on breathing or using guided meditation.

More About Ayurvedic Principles and Optimal Health

You can your boost well-being with herbal support.

- Integrate herbs like turmeric, ashwagandha, and Triphala into your herbal teas or meals to boost immunity and reduce stress.
- Kickstart your mornings with a cup of turmeric or ashwagandha tea for a holistic and nourishing start.
- These calming blends will help set a positive tone for your day, promoting immune health and digestion.

Revitalize with rest and sleep:

- Following natural rhythms, Ayurveda suggests a consistent sleep routine that respects your body's internal clock.
- Create a serene sleep environment with gentle lighting and soothing colors in your bedroom to promote a tranquil atmosphere.
- Relax with a leisurely walk or enjoy calming music.

Keep in mind that Ayurveda promotes a personalized approach. It may be beneficial to seek guidance from an Ayurvedic practitioner to customize these practices according to your specific constitution and requirements.

You've finished. Before you go …

Post/share that you finished this book.

Please star rate this book.

Reviews are solid gold to writers. Please take a few minutes to give us some itty bitty feedback.

ABOUT THE AUTHOR

Gigi Santiago is a dedicated Ayurvedic Practitioner and Integrative Wellness Consultant with a wealth of knowledge and experience in the field. Holding a Master's degree in Ayurveda and Integrative Medicine, she is also a 500-hour Registered Yoga Teacher and a Continuing Education Provider with Yoga Alliance.

Gigi is a teacher's assistant in Ayurveda courses, helping students succeed academically and guiding clients to address their physical and emotional needs for positivity and transformation. Her approach to wellness combines Ayurveda, yoga, and meditation. She emphasizes self-compassion as the key to achieving inner peace and mindfulness. Her holistic method equips clients with tools to manage stress, increase self-awareness, and enhance mental well-being.

Gigi, a Lung Cancer survivor, wife, and mother from Louisville, Kentucky, brings a compassionate and nurturing touch to her practice. Her own journey has equipped her with the understanding and empathy to provide a supportive environment for others on their healing path.

If you enjoyed this Itty Bitty™ book you might also like …

Your Amazing Itty Bitty™ Visibility Book by Dotty Scott

- **Your Amazing Itty Bitty™ Grief Book** by Lisa Y. Herrington

- **Your Amazing Itty Bitty™ Body Life Connection Book** by Suzy Prudden and Joan Meijer Hirschland

Or any of the many Amazing Itty Bitty™ books available online at www.ittybittypublishing.com

www.ingramcontent.com/pod-product-compliance
Lightning Source LLC
Chambersburg PA
CBHW061305040426
42444CB00010B/2533